Soft Skills Sleuths

ETIQUETTE

Investigating Life Skills Success

Diane Lindsey Reeves with Connie Hansen
Illustrations by Ruth Bennett

Cherry Lake Press

Published in the United States of America by Cherry Lake Publishing Group
Ann Arbor, Michigan
www.cherrylakepublishing.com

Created and produced by Bright Futures Press
www.brightfuturespress.com

Reading Advisor: Marla Conn, MS, Ed., Literacy specialist, Read-Ability, Inc.
Illustrator: Ruth Bennett
Cover and Page Designer: Kathy Heming
Design Elements: © mijatmijatovic/Shutterstock.com; © GoodStudio/Shutterstock.com; © Denis Cristo/Shutterstock.com; © Lorelyn Medina/Shutterstock.com; © Yaroshenko Olena/Shutterstock.com; © rangsan paidaen/Shutterstock.com

Cherry Lake Press is an imprint of Cherry Lake Publishing Group.

Library of Congress Cataloging-in-Publication Data has been filed and is available at catalog.loc.gov

Cherry Lake Publishing Group would like to acknowledge the work of the Partnership for 21st Century Learning, a Network of Battelle for Kids. Please visit http://www.battelleforkids.org/networks/p21 for more information.

Printed in the United States of America
Corporate Graphics

TABLE OF CONTENTS

What Are Soft Skills and Why Do I Need Them? 4

Chapter 1 Soft Skill #1: In Public 6

Chapter 2 Soft Skill #2: Online 12

Chapter 3 Soft Skill #3: At the Table 18

Chapter 4 Soft Skill #4: Special Occasions 24

Etiquette Quiz 30

Glossary 31

Index 32

About the Authors 32

About the Illustrator 32

What Are Soft Skills and

Skills are needed to succeed at any job you can imagine. Different jobs require different skills. Professional baseball players need good batting and catching skills. Brain surgeons need steady hands and lots of practice with a scalpel. These are examples of **hard skills** necessary to do specific jobs.

Everyone needs "**soft skills**" to succeed in life. Soft skills get personal. They are about how you behave and treat people. Soft skills are the skills you need to be the very best *you* at home, work, and school.

"Sounds good," you say. "But I don't have a job. Why do I need to worry about soft skills?"

Ahh, but you do have a job. In fact, you have a very important job. You are a student, and your job is to learn as much as you can. Learning soft skills makes you a better student now. It also gets you ready to succeed in any career you choose later.

Etiquette is about talking and acting in ways that show kindness and respect to others. It is what your parents and teachers mean when they ask you to be on your best behavior. Showing good **manners** and being **polite** makes almost any situation you can think of go better.

In this book, you get to be a soft skills **sleuth**. You will track down clues about what good (and not so good!) etiquette looks like. You will **investigate** four situations where etiquette soft skills are in high demand:

- **In public**
- **Online**
- **At the table**
- **Special occasions**

Why Do I Need Them?

HOW TO USE THIS BOOK

Here's how you can be a soft skills sleuth. In each chapter:

- **Gather the facts.** Read the description about the soft skill.
- **Read the case file.** Check out a situation where soft skills are needed.
- **Investigate the case.** Look for clues showing soft skills *successes* and soft skills *mistakes*. Keep track of the clues on a blank sheet of paper.
- **Crack the case.** Did you spot all the clues?

SOFT SKILL #1

Good manners start at home where you treat your family with kindness and respect. When you leave home, make sure to bring your very best manners with you.

Etiquette is all about being polite both at home and in **public**. Polite is the opposite of rude. Being polite means talking and acting in ways that consider other people's feelings. Rude people don't care about **offending** others. They make others feel bad. Good manners bring out the best in everyone.

Polite words like "please," "thank you," and "excuse me" play a role in good manners. Actions like smiling and saying hello, holding a door open for someone, or offering your seat on a crowded bus to someone all show good manners.

How many times have you heard parents remind a small child to use good manners? "What do you say, sweetie?" they might ask. They do this because good manners do not come naturally. That's why you need to practice them until they become a habit.

Good manners come with a guarantee. You always feel good when you use them. Other people always feel good when they receive them.

Mind Your Manners

- Treat others how you want to be treated.
- Be on time.
- Think before you speak.
- Knock on closed doors.
- Cover your mouth when coughing or sneezing.
- Look people in the eye when speaking to them.
- Apologize when you mess up.
- Avoid calling people mean names.

"Politeness and consideration for others is like investing pennies and getting dollars back."
—Thomas Sowell

IN PUBLIC

SOFT SKILLS CASE #1: IN PUBLIC

Your school is hosting the National Quiz Bowl Championships. Teams from four states are battling it out for this academic competition. It's a big deal, and the pressure is on each player to do their best. Lots of people are cheering them on.

All the teams brought smart answers. But are they using good manners to share their smarts in this very public place? May the best manners win!

DO:
Investigate in public successes and mistakes!

DO NOT:
Write in this book!

The teams and their fans in the audience want to get this right. Who wins the prize for most impressive manners in a public place?

THE WINNING ANSWER IS ETIQUETTE

IN PUBLIC

Good manners are the answer. What was the question?

Did you find all the successes and MISTAKES?

Start here!

Mistake.
Losing your cool and leaving your team in the lurch.

Success!
Hurray for the home team!

Mistake.
Making a mess of the place.

Success!
Taking your turn, answering clearly.

CASE NOTES

Bring your best manners with you wherever you go.

Success!
Working together.

Did you find them all?

Mistake.
What's with the kid under the table with the answer book?

Success!
Treating teammates with respect.

Mistake.
Interrupting the speaker.

Mistake.
It's time to win, not time to eat!

SOFT SKILL #2

Smartphones. Tablets. Laptops. All this technology has changed the way people keep in touch. Write a letter to a faraway friend, and it takes days for the mail to reach them. **Text** or **email** someone anywhere in the world, and they receive it in a matter of seconds.

Technology makes communication simpler. It also makes it more complicated. It is a little too easy to fire off an angry message without waiting to cool down. If you wouldn't say or show something in person, don't say or show it **online**.

Messages meant to be private can go public with just a click of a button. Once your words and images go out into **cyberspace**, it can be very difficult to take them back. You lose control of who sees your information. In other words, no secret is safe online.

Making poor choices online can have big consequences. What if your future boss looks you up online? If they find rude or irresponsible behavior in your social media accounts, they will not hire you. Using bad manners online can result in you missing out on opportunities and messing up friendships.

Think before you text, **tweet**, or email. Online etiquette keeps digital communication fun and safe.

Netiquette: Etiquette for the Internet

- Follow cyber safety rules about privacy, passwords, and kid-friendly content.
- Never share private information with a stranger online.
- Don't ever bully, stalk, or embarrass someone online.
- Make sure your posts are okay for parents, teachers, and future bosses to see.

"Think before you click."
—Germany Kent

ONLINE

SOFT SKILLS CASE #2: ONLINE

Today is the deadline for the latest issue of the school newspaper. The newspaper club is working hard to wrap up stories and get images to fill the pages with the latest news. Cell phones and emails make it easier to get the scoop. Are these young journalists using good online manners to get the job done?

DO:
Investigate online successes and mistakes!

DO NOT:
Write in this book!

YOU HEARD IT HERE FIRST

The newspaper club is eager to share the school's headline news. What's the scoop about their online etiquette?

ONLINE

The new issue of the school paper is due tomorrow. Will their online etiquette meet the deadline?

Did you find all the successes and MISTAKES?

Start here!

Mistake.
Too much technology (like overflowing inboxes) can be too much.

Success!
Smile and say "cheese" while I snap this prize-winning photo.

Mistake.
Watch those snarky text messages!

Success!
Online chats can be lots of fun when you mind your manners.

CASE NOTES

Think twice before you text, email, or post images online.

Success!
Good cell phone manners matter.

Did you find them all?

Mistake.
Be careful not to bug other people with too much cell phone chatter.

Mistake.
Sorry, there's no room for selfies in this week's paper.

Success!
Use the same good manners in emails that you would use in letters.

SOFT SKILL #3

Few things in life are as fun as sharing a meal with good friends. It gives you a chance to talk and relax while enjoying yummy foods. Think of good **table manners** as an insurance policy. They make it possible for everyone to enjoy the meal. It is a sign of **civility** when people choose to act in a way that makes it easy for others to enjoy their company.

It doesn't matter if you are at home with your family or at a restaurant with friends, bad table manners are just gross. Good table manners are a kindness you share with others. You're following a set of rules about things you should and shouldn't do while eating. For instance, you shouldn't reach across someone to grab food. You should ask for food to be passed. Once you've got the rules down, it is easy to follow them.

Just stay calm, take your time, and enjoy those around you. When in doubt, watch someone who has good table manners and do what they do.

Table Manners Do's and Don'ts

- DO chew with your mouth closed.
- DO use your napkin.
- DO wait until you're done chewing to take a drink.
- DO ask for food to be passed to you instead of reaching across the table for it.
- DON'T use your phone at the table.
- DON'T pick your teeth at the table.
- DON'T slouch or put your elbows on the table while eating.
- DON'T burp, blow your nose, or make rude noises at the table.

"Good manners are just a way of showing other people that we have respect for them."
—Bill Kelly

AT THE TABLE

SOFT SKILLS CASE #3: AT THE TABLE

It's the school sports banquet. Everyone has gathered for a special meal to celebrate the school's star athletes. The students are enjoying good food and fun with their friends. Some of them are making it easy for people nearby to enjoy their meal by using good table manners. Others seem to have left their good table manners at home. Can you tell which ones are which?

DO:
Investigate at the table successes and mistakes!

DO NOT:
Write in this book!

PLEASE PASS THE TABLE MANNERS

The school is celebrating all their athletes. Are these students rising to the occasion by using their all-star table manners?

AT THE TABLE

Eating together can be lots of fun. Whose bad table manners are spoiling the good time?

Did you **find** all the successes and **MISTAKES**?

Start here!

Success!
Using your fork, knife, and spoon correctly.

Mistake.
Talking with food in your mouth.

Success!
Talking nicely with friends at your table.

Success!
Helping a friend get seated.

CASE NOTES

Mistake. Making a big mess.

Mistake. Slurping your drink.

Are good table manners on your menu?

Did you find them all?

Success! Passing bowls of food to the person on your right.

Success! Would you like some more water?

Mistake. Hey! Save some food for the rest of us.

SOFT SKILL #4

The invitation has been accepted. You're wearing a great new outfit bought just for this day. Now it's time to make the most of this **special occasion**. Just be sure your manners match the reason for the event. Your behavior will, of course, be different for a wedding than it is for a funeral. It will be different for a big birthday bash than for a student conference.

Some events call for a serious, quiet approach. Others for focus and cooperation. Many call for outright, "let's get this party started" celebration! All special occasions are better when people behave themselves properly. Being able to "read the room" and get this right is a valuable soft skill to learn.

The basic rules of good manners are always the same. Speak politely. Respect other people and their property. Be helpful and kind. You can't go wrong with these manners no matter where you are.

The thing to ask yourself is this: Am I doing anything that prevents other people from enjoying the event? If the answer is yes, then stop it! If the answer is no, then relax and lean into the purpose of the event.

Tips for Extra-Special Etiquette

- If an invitation says "RSVP," it means "please respond." Let your host know if you can or can't attend.
- Dress appropriately for the event.
- Ask an adult to describe what to expect in new types of situations.
- Get there on time.
- Follow the cues of other people who are behaving properly.
- Be mindful of how you treat others around you.

"Etiquette requires us to admire the human race."
—Mark Twain

SPECIAL OCCASIONS

SOFT SKILLS CASE #4: SPECIAL OCCASIONS

Students are not usually included in PTA meetings. But this is a special occasion. The student council was invited to the meeting to share ideas about a new cafeteria courtyard. It's their chance to explain why giving students an outdoor space to relax during lunchtime is a good idea. If the meeting goes well, the PTA will donate funds to build the courtyard.

This is the student council's big chance. They don't want anything—or anyone—to mess things up. Are the students' manners making a good impression on the PTA? Turn the page and find out.

DO:
Investigate special occasions successes and mistakes!

DO NOT:
Write in this book!

COURTING SUPPORT FOR A STUDENT COURTYARD

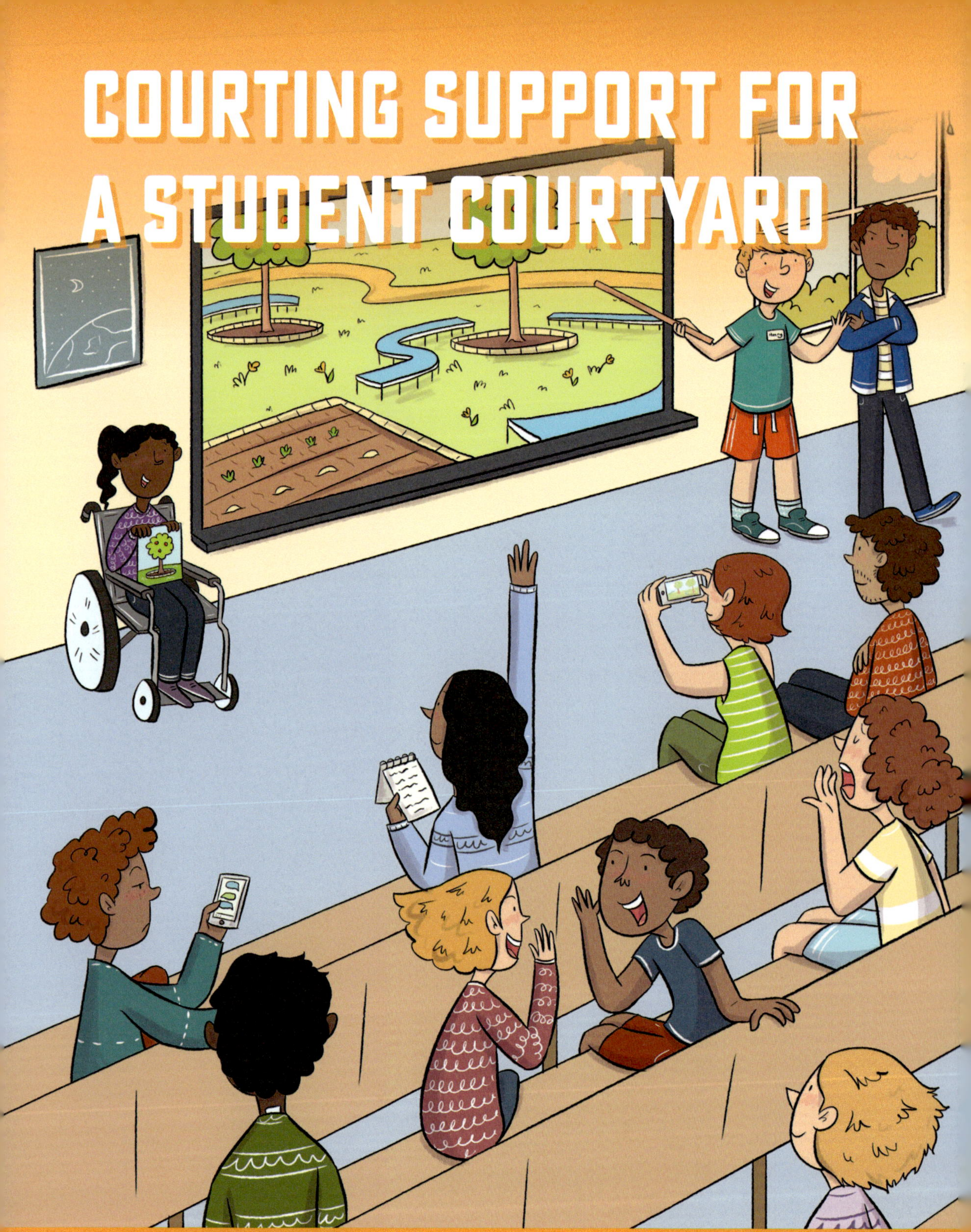

It's a special occasion to present a special request. Will the students' special occasion etiquette help or hurt their cause?

SPECIAL OCCASIONS

Good manners are making the case for a student courtyard. Will they impress the PTA?

Start here!

Success!
Raising hand to ask a question.

Mistake.
Interrupting the conversation by yelling out comments.

Success!
Listening politely to the discussion.

Mistake.
How about turning off that cell phone!

Did you find all the successes and MISTAKES?

CASE NOTES

Special occasions call for extra-special manners.

Mistake. Chatting with your neighbor.

Did you find them all?

Mistake. Forget the courtyard! We want more vending machines.

Success! Giving a well-prepared and polite presentation (with visuals).

Success! Encouraging the speakers to do a good job.

WHAT HAVE YOU Learned?

ETIQUETTE QUIZ

Question 1:

____________ is another way of saying good manners.

Question 2:

____________ manners make other people feel good, while ____________ manners make them feel bad.

Question 3:

Letters sent by mail can take days to receive; ____________ and ____________ are received in seconds.

Question 4:

Secrets are not safe ____________.

Question 5:

Do ____________ with your mouth closed; don't talk with your mouth ____________.

Question 6:

Good table manners are a ____________ you share with others.

Question 7:

Good manners are based on a set of ____________ .

Question 8:

____________ on an invitation means "please respond."

ANSWERS

1. *Etiquette*
2. *Polite or Good, rude or bad*
3. *Emails, texts*
4. *online or in cyberspace*
5. *chew, full*
6. *kindness*
7. *rules*
8. *RSVP*

Etiquette soft skills start here!

GLOSSARY

civility (suh-VIL-ih-tee) the act of showing regard for others by being polite

cyberspace (SYE-bur-spase) the world of communication and interaction represented by the internet

email (EE-mayl) to send electronic messages to people through a computer network or over the internet

etiquette (ET-ih-kit) the formal manners and rules that are followed in social or professional settings

hard skills (HAHRD SKILZ) specific skills needed to do a specific job

investigate (in-VES-tih-gate) to gather information or clues about something

manners (MAN-urz) polite behavior

online (awn-LINE) connected to or controlled by a central computer or system of computers

polite (puh-LITE) being well-behaved and courteous to others

public (PUHB-lik) all the places people go that are outside their homes

sleuth (SLOOTH) a detective, or person who is good at finding facts and clues

soft skills (SAWFT SKILZ) behaviors and personality traits people use every day to succeed in life

special occasion (SPESH-uhl uh-KAY-zhuhn) significant event, especially a large or important social gathering

table manners (TAY-buhl MAN-urz) good behavior while eating a meal at a table

text (TEKST) to send messages to people using a cell phone

tweet (TWEET) to post messages on the social media application Twitter

INDEX

birthday, 24
conference, 24
cyberspace, 12
email, 12
funeral, 24
Kelly, Bill, 18
Kent, Germany, 12
polite, 6
rude, 6
Sowell, Thomas, 6
text, 12
Twain, Mark, 24
tweet, 12
wedding, 24

ABOUT THE AUTHORS

Diane Lindsey Reeves likes to write books that help students figure out what they want to be when they grow up. She mostly lives in Washington, D.C., but spends as much time as she can in North Carolina and South Carolina with her grandkids.

Connie Hansen spent 25 years teaching college students about successful life skills. She lives in Lynchburg, Virginia where her favorite thing to do is play with her grandchildren. Her happy place is the beach!

ABOUT THE ILLUSTRATOR

Ruth Bennett lives in a small country village in the heart of Norfolk, England, with her two cats, Queen Elizabeth and Queen Victoria. She loves petting dogs, watching movies, and drawing, of course!